365 Days
of Creative Writing

Rosemary Augustine

Barbara
Thank you for
all your love and
support over the years
Enjoy
Love & hugs
Rosemary
2012

DEDICATION

This book is dedicated to my parents, Ernest and Rose Augustine. Each taught me skills that I have used throughout my life both as an entrepreneur and a woman. My father was a musician and successful entrepreneur who followed his passion until the day he died. My mother was very creative at various times in her life. They each taught me valuable lessons of perseverance and independence - each from their own perspective. I am most grateful to each of them for their love and lessons throughout my life even today.

INTRODUCTION

What Is Creative Writing?

For me, creative writing is just about any kind of writing - fiction or non-fiction; poetry or prose, sci-fi, mysteries, bio's and more. Even letters and business correspondence can sometimes come from a creative spark using writing as the base. Simply stated, creative writing gives you the inspiration your need to write in these genres and more.

When writing outside the bounds of journalistic or academic literature, you write "outside the box" with no right or wrong way of writing - loose, free and with a "stream of consciousness," letting the writing flow from you freely and easily. This gives you a foundation for building your writing projects.

How Does Creative Writing Work?

As a writer, creative writing stretches my imagination with thoughts, ideas, prompts and free writing exercises that then may develop into an article, blog, newsletter, chapter or even a book. With creative writing, I've created my own writing style, and I'm never at a loss for words - whether writing at 6 AM or midnight. I am writing and that's what is important.

Creative writing offers a chance to write when blocked, write when troubled, write when happy and write for no reason at all. Writing tells a story, helps identify patterns, resolve issues, provide personal and professional growth and more - all through using creative writing as part of the process.

How Do I Use The Prompts In This Book?

The prompts in this book are designed to spark ideas, thoughts and inspiration. Pick a prompt, write about the thoughts or inspiration the prompt creates for you. Let the writing flow and don't be concerned if your writing takes you off task of the prompt you selected. It's OK. Remember, there is no right or wrong way to the creative writing process. Your daily prompt writings should last about 5-15 minutes. If you are concerned for time, set a timer for 15 minutes and start writing.

Some of the prompts may be interpreted as metaphors. Words like garden, road trip, trucks, etc. can be interesting prompts when used as metaphors. Weeding your garden may include weeding out the things (and maybe even relationships) that no longer serve you in your life. You may also find ongoing themes - word prompts that are repeated several times yet offering different suggested inspiration. What's most important is you don't analyze the prompt. Read it, re-read it and listen to your inner voice. Begin to write what your inner voice is saying.

Writing your response to these prompts may take anywhere from 5-15 minutes. My recommended timeframe includes setting a timer as mentioned above. Part of the creative writing process is getting lost as you write, while still enjoying yourself. If you spend too much time on one prompt - writing for an hour let's say - you may become discouraged, angry, and feel that writing is taking too much time.

If you are using any of these prompts to work on characters, plots, background, outlines, etc., write as described and also use a highlighter indicating certain key words or subject matter to refer back to later. Always put your subject at the top of the page. If you are keeping your pages electronically, have different "subject" folders for your writing files.

I Have Writers Block, So Can These Prompts Help Me?

The list of reasons why we don't write is endless. Here are some writing blocks that I have heard over time with recommended information following this list. I only included a few excuses:

- I'd rather do this: on the computer… on the train… before I go to bed… Or (finish this statement).

- I can't decide if I should write or draw.

- Mornings are not my best time… do I have to write only in the morning?

- I can't suddenly "be creative" or "turn on" my writing, so I'll just wait until I am creative.

- It takes a lot for me to sit and write.

- I can only write when I travel or when I'm away from home.

- I don't have time today, maybe later, and later never comes.

- I can't decide whether to use plain, lined or graph paper… or my computer.

- I can't decide the size of the journal or notebook.

Don't get caught up in these traps that block your writing. It doesn't matter what you write on, when or where you write or whether it's a bound or spiral notebook or created electronically. What matters is that you write. Set a timer and get the pen moving.

For more involved writing projects that you need continued inspiration (such as a book, its chapters and/or character development), find your peak creative time of day, and again set a timer. This time set it for at least 55 - 95 minutes and when that timer signals your time is up, finish your thoughts and wrap up.

You ask, "When is my peak creative time of day?" You will have to experiment with this. But do experiment, and once you find it, use that time to your writing advantage.

Throughout the day, be aware that additional inspiration will surface. As it does, you will need to capture the words, phrases or stream of consciousness in order to remember it. So keep a small notebook with you (and always carry a pen). Keep a small notebook and pen by your bed as well. If you find you don't capture these thoughts when they surface, they will be lost deep in your sub-conscious and impossible to retrieve at a later time.

Can I Do These Prompts As Part of My Daily Journal?

Journaling is about writing as well. Though, your daily journaling practice should be written only on paper, using a pen or favorite writing instrument. It doesn't matter if the paper is lined, plain or graph - just write! The healing properties of journaling go well beyond the written word and provide a catharsis of areas in your life needing repair, change or growth. Journaling is not thinking the words nor is it about writing your thoughts using a computer keyboard.

By actually putting pen to paper, you create a stream of consciousness that directs you to answers (and more), deep inside you. You would never attain such answers just by verbalizing them or by keyboarding your thoughts. You can also paint, sketch or create an art journal or life journal that has similar results as with writing long hand. Daily journaling is best when done early in the morning before any distractions of the day filter into your life. If you are at a loss for words at 6:15 AM, then this book is perfect, as it provides you ongoing prompts any day of the year. You can also jot thoughts, words, or observations on a sticky note throughout the day and later paste into your journal for writing ideas or thoughts to journal on another day.

What Will I Gain If I Use These Prompts For Daily Journaling?

Use the prompts for ideas, inspiration, provoking thought, memories and healing areas of your life. Here are just a few things you will gain from a daily journaling practice:

- You begin to get in touch with who you truly are – your true self;

- You also start to tap into your inner voice – whether supportive or critical;

- With journaling, you can learn to create support and silence your inner critic;

- Journaling generates self-introspection, addressing fears, issues and ongoing patterns;

- A daily journal becomes a form of personal self – expression by using writing and/or sketching;

- Journaling creates a conscious awareness of values, life, blocks, patterns, choices, consequences, etc.

- Writing in a journal will help you uncover positive and negative self-talk – including yours and others, directed toward you or others.

- Regular journaling helps you discover the things that you may need to change in your life and gives you the strength to make those changes;

- Journaling will also provide you a process to work through any changes before you physically make those changes;

- Journaling will give you a clearer picture of where you want to go and how to get there.

These are only a few things you can gain with daily journaling. Those who journal regularly and consistently find it a very valuable friend. Have a favorite pen and a special place that you go to when journaling... maybe a favorite chair or a special room. Find what inspires you. If you are distracted, then listen to that message and write about your distraction. When you write, listen to your inner voice since it has important messages for you when using creative writing as part of your daily journaling.

I Am Worried That Someone Will Find My Journal Writings and Read It.

Let me first say, if you are not writing out of fear of someone else finding your most private thoughts, then all the more reason to write. There is a hidden message here; please heed it. There is tremendous emotional healing and personal growth that comes with creative writing - whether writing a blog, book or having a daily journaling practice. Your emotions need to surface and be addressed. The longer you wait to heal those emotions, the deeper they are buried and ultimately creating physical illness for you. Write, please, for your own health - mental, spiritual, physical, emotional and more.

So I leave you to enjoy this book. Please let *365 Days of Creative Writing* be a companion for you regardless of your level of writing. I created this work to inspire you, to give you ideas when you've run out of them, and to provoke thought for those times when you may over-think a process. Feel free to use the blank space on each page for notes, writing ideas, memories or even an opportunity to sketch.

Please enjoy! Creating this book gave me great joy knowing you would be inspired.

Rosemary Augustine, Author and Journal Aficionado

1

FIRST

Journal about your "Firsts."
The first time, arriving first, being first.

2

DIFFERENCE

Journal on how you use your time and talents,
to make a positive difference in the lives of others.

3

DISTRACTIONS

Identify your distractions
and how they redirect your true focus.

4

ANNOYANCES

Journal on annoyances
and how to resolve such annoyances from your life.

5

TOLERANCE

Journal beyond annoyances
and look deeper into
your unacceptable level of tolerance.

6

DISTRACTIONS

What distractions are in your life
that need to be addressed? List all of them.

7

SMILE

Dig deep and find a reason to smile.
Share that smile with everyone you meet today.

8

LAUGHTER

Today I will include laughter as part of my journey.

9

LAUGH

Today I will take a moment
and make someone else laugh.

10

LAUGHTER

Tell a joke to generate deep belly laughter,
for yourself and others.

11

LAUGHTER

What a great day to write about how laughter affects your body!

12

CHANGE

Time to change addictive behavior in your life.
Journal on what life would be like addiction free.

13

BLUES

Feeling the blues? Are you shopping for white sales, a warming trend or looking for the music?

14

SING

Pick your favorite song, and sing it all day long.

.

15

DANCE

Take every opportunity to dance today.

16

LIFE

Never confuse having a job with having a life!
Do you have a life?

17

BELIEVE

Today I believe strongly in who I am,
and ground myself in faith and belief in spirit.

18

SUNNY DAY

Offer a sunny day to someone,
regardless of the weather.

19

TOXINS

What toxins do you want to make others aware of?

20

TOXINS

I found turpentine oil, shellac and petroleum
in products that we use and ingest daily!
What toxins did you find today?

21

AWARENESS

Read labels, signs and ingredient lists to pay attention, and become aware of what's really healthy.

22

INGREDIENTS

What foods offer you simple ingredients?
My rule of thumb: I don't eat foods that have
ingredients I can't pronounce or define.

23

SPICE

Beyond salt and pepper, name your favorite spice.
What dishes do you include this spice in regularly?

24

SPICE

Write a short story
in which you are the spice in the dish of life.

25

SALT

Describe how salt is part of life, such as:
salt of the earth, road salt, salt shaker,
sweet and salty or other salt phrases.

Write about which one you relate to in your life.

26

LIKES

The things you don't like in others,
are really the things you don't like in yourself!

27

LAUGH

Laugh at yourself before you laugh at others today.
Journal on your feelings around this.

28

LAUGHTER

Journal on the important role
laughter has played in your life.

29

SPIRIT DAY

Take today as a Spirit Day and be alone with your thoughts. Journal on your negative thoughts and how to make them positive thoughts in your life.

30

REJOICE

Journal on the word "Rejoice" and what it means,
the role it plays,
and the places you see it in your life.

31

THINGS

Make a list of 6 things you've never done
and would like to complete in the next 30 days.
Now pick 3 ... and schedule how and when
you will complete them.

32

THINGS

Take the remaining 3 things from the previous exercise and see how you can incorporate those 3 things into your life ... before the end of the year.

33

CLEARING SPACE

Journal on letting go of the old
and clearing space for the new.

34

ACTIVITIES

What activities continue to distract, interrupt and/or interfere with your daily life of being?

35

WAITING

Are you: waiting, preparing and being?
Or waiting, preparing and doing?

36

WHAT MIGHT BE?

Anticipation, excitement, or fear of what might be?
So... what might be?

37

MOTHER

A reminder of mother nature and her fury.

38

STORMS

Remember stormy times in your life.
What characteristics brought you through
those stormy times?

39

NAVIGATING

How do you navigate your way
to smooth sailing after the storm?

40

BE

Learning to BE while waiting for the storm to pass.

41

CHANGE

With change comes fear and a need for commitment.
What are some changes you will commit to?

42

POSSIBILITIES

What are all the possibilities coming your way?

43

OPEN

How do you stay open to all the possibilities?

44

HEART

Meditate on your heart, and listen to the beat.
Get in touch with your heart's desire.

45

LISTEN

What has your heart been telling you lately?

46

LOVE

Describe your love as a many splendored thing.

47

FLOWER

Journal as your favorite flower.

48

SATISFIED

Imagine what your life would be like
if you were satisfied with what you have,
rather than what you want.

49

FULL GLASS

Describe how your life would be
if you viewed life as the glass that is always full.

50

WARMTH

In the deep of winter,
reach inside and find your inner warmth.

51

PERMISSION

Give yourself permission to experience joy.
Describe the feeling.

52

FRUSTRATION

I am no longer frustrated because...
(finish this statement).

53

HAPPY

Today I am happy because...
(finish this statement).

54

HAPPY

Today I will make someone else happy by...
(finish this statement).

55

SUNSHINE

Today the sun is shining inside and out,
making happiness a...
(finish this statement).

56

HAPPINESS

Happiness for me is defined as...
(finish this statement).

57

HAPPY

Journal on who makes you happy.

58

HAPPY

Sing to yourself happy songs,
using the word "happy" in the lyrics.

59

HAPPY

Today, take yourself on a happy date - doing something or going somewhere that makes you happy.

60

PERFECT

Describe how "Perfect" interferes with enjoying life.

61

BONUS

Pick your own topic, or write about the word "Bonus."

62

SILENCE

Take the day and be silent.
Do not talk,
not even a whisper.

63

SILENCE

If every thing has a shape
and every shape has a sound,
what shape is silence?

64

OPEN

What have you received lately
because you are more open?

65

GIVING

Life is about giving.
What do you give to others,
the world, the universe?

66

INSPIRATION

Who inspires you? Who do you inspire?

67

JOY

Take today and celebrate joy -
yours and others!

68

PLEASANT

Make today pleasant for yourself and others.
Journal on the process of "Pleasant."

69

CORE

Journal today on finding your core essence.

70

INSPIRE

Write about how you inspire others to be their best.

71

DELIGHT

Journal about all the places you find delight.

72

COMFORT

What can you do to stretch
beyond your comfort zone today?

73

IMMERSE

Immerse yourself
in whatever you choose to write about today!

74

DELIGHT

Take today and journal about when you
found delight in your life.

75

REFLECT

Today I reflect on the light in my life.

76

MIRROR

Write a story about the mirror.
What do you see?

77

POSSIBILITIES

Write about all the possibilities -
but only in the present.

78

GREEN

Today, are we green with envy
or green with celebration?

79

MYSTERY

What mystery do you find needs to be resolved?

80

MAGIC

Find the magic in today's chaos.
Journal about the magic.

8 1

PLAY

Take time today to play...
and, later write a story about your play day.

82

OBSERVATION

Observe people, places, nature, and more.
Write a short story about what you observed today.

83

GIFT

Today is a gift! Write about your gift.

84

TASK

What impossible task have you mastered?
Write about your achievement,
and how you made it happen.

85

JUGGLING

Record your technique in juggling a more than full plate.
Does something need to move off?

86

SACRIFICE

Journal about the sacrifice others have made
to make you happy.

87

GENUINE

Journal about being genuine -
you or others.

88

PUZZLE

Today, find a puzzle, and work it to completion.

89

SPIRIT

Free write today about finding spirit...
and living spiritually.

90

BRIDGE

Crossing, using, avoiding...
free write about a bridge in your life.

91

CONQUESTS

Chronicle your childhood conquests, including...
(finish this statement).

92

BULLET

Once again I dodged a bullet.
Write about this experience.

93

INVESTIGATE

When I investigate...
(finish this statement).

94

CONSTRUCTION

I am no longer in the construction zone...
(finish this statement).

95

SUNSHINE

Journal about how you find sunshine on a rainy day.
Include examples and your feelings.

96

CHANGE

Describe how change is a major part of your life.

97

RESTRICTIONS

List all the restrictions in your life
and how those restrictions became part of your life.

98

FEAR

Describe how fear motivates or paralyzes you.

99

LIMITS

What limits have you placed on yourself,
your life, relationships, career?

100

SUCCESS

Define your recipe for success.

101

LESSON

What valuable lesson did you learn today?

102

ACCOMPLISHMENTS

Say to yourself,
"I really have accomplished great things."
Write about 3 of them.

103

CHALLENGE

Today I am no longer challenged by...
(finish this statement).

104

ADVENTURE

Seek out an adventure and write about it.

105

THOUGHTS

"I may not write often,
however, you are often in my thoughts."
Write a letter to someone you've lost touch with.
It's your option whether or not to mail it.

106

PROCRASTINATION

Record all the things that you procrastinate about
and how you can break your pattern of procrastination.

107

PROCRASTINATE

List 10 reasons why you will no longer procrastinate.

108

BALANCE

How does balance keep you steady
when others fail to see the importance of balance?

109

CEILING

What happens when you hit the ceiling?
Write about those feelings.

110

LIMITS

What limits have you imposed on yourself?
By writing an affirmation, release those limits.

111

LIMITS

Describe how your life would be when living your life with no limits.

112

LOVE

If you were to do what you love...
what do you love?

113

PURPOSE

Describe purpose
and what you feel is your purpose.

114

MEANING

Write about the life of meaning,
rather than the meaning of life.

115

REASON

What is your reason for being,
doing, creating? Write about all 3.

116

SKY

What can you do
to make the sky your limit?

117

VISION

Create a vision statement projecting 5-10 years.

118

DISCOVER

Take time today to discover something new.

119

RISK

Write about a time you risked it all.

120

VALUE

Record your favorite thoughts about something
that is valuable to you.

1 2 1

ALWAYS

Journal about something that always happens to you and why you think it does.

122

DREAMS

Think positive, dream big!
Write about why you would consider dreaming small?

123

JOY

Chronicle all the joy in your life.

124

PERFECT

Describe your perfect day.

125

TRANSFORM

Transform yourself today
into someone you would like to be.

126

SURPRISE

What has happened in your life
that had a surprise ending?

127

ZOOM ALONG

Describe your life
as you zoom along the highway of life.

128

SPEED

At what speed would you like to travel through life?

129

PATIENCE

Write a letter to yourself
from a friend's point of view,
describing your patience.

130

MOM

Write about how your mother
did or did not influence your life.

131

MOM

Thoughts of your mom or of being a mom.

132

FLOWER

Create a story about you as your favorite flower,
include all the elements of color and bloom stages.

133

FRIENDS

Describe your friends as flowers,
and include all the elements
of color and bloom stages.

134

GARDEN

Describe your life as a garden.

135

PESTS

Identify any garden pests,
and define their role in your garden.

136

SKETCH

Sketch your garden today,
regardless of your artistic skills.

137

GRADUATION

Celebrate graduation!
Chronicle any situation that created an opportunity
to advance regardless of education.

138

FAREWELL

Journal about a time you bid farewell.

139

ANGER

Journal on your anger and how you can resolve your anger toward positive productivity.

140

RESISTANCE

We resist that which we need the most.
What are you resisting?

141

RESENTMENT

What role is resentment playing in your life?

142

LOSS

Chronicle the toll personal loss
has played in your life.

143

LOSS

Journal on the positive and negative
aspects of your loss.

144

TEARS

Whatever hurts needs to be washed away with tears.

145

HEART

Write a letter to your heart,
describing your promise to heal it.

146

RESPECT

Write about respect...
for yourself, elders, strangers,
animals, elements, emotions, and more.

147

HONOR

Begin to honor those you lost.

148

REMEMBRANCE

Take time to remember loved ones.

149

THOUGHTS

Recognize the power of your thoughts -
both positive and negative.

150

RENEW

What steps do you take
to renew your spirit regularly?

151

SELF

Describe your self-care methods.

152

CENTER

Outline your journey to center - your inner balance.

153

BALANCE

Describe how you achieve balance in your life.

154

PICK A TOPIC

Write about the one topic you know best.

155

SURVIVOR

Journal on your role as a survivor.

156

GRIEF

Describe how you gave yourself permission
to grieve a loss.

157

WRITE

Write a message to your heart.

158

WRITE

Write your obituary describing your accomplishments
(even those not yet achieved).

159

TRADITIONS

What are your traditions, symbols or family rituals associated with water?

160

WATER

Journal on how water reflects light and beauty.

161

REFLECTION

Write about the word "Reflection"
and its meaning in your life at this time.

162

SAILING

Write about your experience with smooth sailing,
when you hit rough seas
and how you eventually returned to smooth sailing.

163

DROWNING

Do you feel as if you are drowning?
Write about why you feel that way in your life.

164

TEARS

Describe a time you experienced tears of joy.

165

FEET

Soak your feet! Sit quietly while you do this,
and savor the feeling of relaxation.

166

TRIP

Time for a road trip!
Journal about where you are going.

167

TRUCKS

The road trip of life includes trucks. Tell me more.

168

ROADS

On your road trip of life,
what new roads are being explored?

169

CONSTANT

As you travel on your road trip of life,
what seems to be a constant?

170

OBVIOUS

As you journal throughout your road trip, recognize the
obvious and determine any new directions.

171

JOURNEY

Journal about your journey, not your destination.

172

DAD

Write about how your father influenced your life.

173

DAD

Thoughts of your dad or on being a dad.

174

LIGHT

How will you enjoy the longest day of the year?

175

PLANTING

In tending to your garden of life,
how well are the seeds growing that you planted?

176

WEEDS

What weeds need to be pulled from the garden?

177

GARDEN

What nourishment needs to be added to your garden?

178

GARDEN

What activities stimulate garden growth?

179

GARDEN

What do you value most in your garden?

180

GARDEN

What garden invaders need to be eradicated?

181

SUMMER VACATION

Journal about your summer vacation -
wishes, wants and expectations.

182

TENSION

Your summer vacation is designed to release tension.
Journal about this tension.

183

RELAX

Finally you are starting to relax on vacation.
Journal about your relaxed feelings.

184

VISIT

Your summer vacation included
a visit to................? Write about this visit.

185

ENJOYMENT

What things brought you enjoyment on your vacation?

186

REFRESHED

What refreshed you the most this week?

187

FREEDOM

Describe what freedom means to you.

188

FREEDOM

If freedom was a color,
what color would you assign to freedom.

189

LISTEN

Listen to nature. What do you hear?
How many different sounds do you hear at once?

190

TAKE A MINUTE

Stop and notice your surroundings.
Write about what you see.

191

OBSERVATION

What have you observed today?
Include how you used your senses.

192

BUTTERFLIES

Observe the flight of butterflies,
and write about your observation.

193

NATURE

If you could be part of nature,
what part would you be?

194

SPIRIT

Describe what you do to replenish your spirit?

195

DIRT

Write about your childhood memories
and playing in the dirt.

196

MEMORIES

What memories do you have about sand castles?

197

SAND CASTLES

Write a fairy tale about building a sand castle,
with you as the main character.

198

GOALS

Write a list in your journal of
10 goals you wish to complete this year.

199

ACTION

What is needed to take specific action
toward your goals?

200

FOUNDATION

Describe the strength of your foundation.

201

WRITE

Write a letter to a special friend,
updating them on your life.
Use ink and fancy paper ... and mail it!

202

WRITE

Write a letter to yourself
about something you lost and never found again.

203

COMMUNICATION

What role does non-verbal communication
play in your relationships?

204

HEALING

The road to healing is a long one.
Outline your steps needed to begin healing.

205

HEALING

Describe how journaling is an open door
to healing your heart and soul.

206

GUILT

Spend a few minutes writing about why guilt overpowers your ability to move forward.

207

DEATH

Death is so final... write about your final good-byes.

208

DYING

Journal on your fear of death and dying.

209

DECEPTION

What role does deception play
in self-sabotaging yourself?

210

GOD

Define your interpretation of god.

211

GOD

Describe how god influences your life.

212

GOD

If there is no god, then... (finish this statement).

213

GOD

God failed me when... (finish this statement).

214

GOD

God shows s/he loves me when...
(finish this statement).

215

HIDE

Describe your secret hide-a-way.

216

SECRETS

Journal about the secrets you are keeping.

217

SECRET

If you were the best kept secret,
where would you hide?

218

SECRET

What secret do you wish you had kept secret?

219

SECRET

Write in depth about unlocking
the secret to your heart.

220

SECRETS

Secrets hidden or secrets revealed...
which one for you today?

221

CLOSENESS

"Closeness has nothing to do with distance."
(From an unknown author).
Write about closeness.

222

GOD

How do you replenish your spirit with god?

223

PASSION

Be passionate about something,
and make it your life's work.
What is your passion?

224

GOD

What role does god play in your life?

225

INTENTIONS

Describe your intentions for your life's plan.

226

DOG DAYS

Describe your dog days of summer -
by days or by daze.

227

INTENTIONS

What intentions does god have in mind for you?
Dialogue with god in your journal.

228

INTENTIONS

Set your real intention for a new year's resolution.

229

STILLNESS

Write about stillness, quiet, and whispers today.

230

BREATH

Catch your breath and write about your experience.

231

POEM

Write a poem describing when
something took your breath away.

232

BREATHLESS

Journal about a time when
you had your breath taken away.

233

AWARENESS

Sit still and listen to your breathing.

234

AIR

Does any particular memory come to mind?

235

PROMISE

Write a letter to yourself
about a whisper or promise
that you promised to keep.

236

WHISPER

If you whisper today, what would you say?

237

ACTION

Whenever I take action... (complete this phrase).

238

AWARENESS

Describe how the awareness of god affects you.

239

AWARENESS

Raise your awareness level today,
and be alert for change.

240

ANGER

Describe your anger as a mirror to resentment.

241

ANGER

When I'm angry, I... (complete this phrase).

242

BE

Be still today and listen for signals.

243

BALANCE

Describe your balance
in relation to the bigger scheme of things.

244

BUTTERFLIES

If only I could flit around and...
(finish this statement).

245

LOVE

Describe how you give your best love.

246

TODAY

Today, write with your non-dominant hand.

247

CELEBRATION

Today find a reason to celebrate.
Journal about your celebration.

248

CONNECTION

Link together how you know everyone.
What is the connection?

249

COLOR

Write with both hands simultaneously,
each with a different color pen.

250

FEAR

What is your greatest fear?

251

FEAR

Write about what you feel is the opposite of fear.

252

MIRROR

How does mirroring affect your life?

253

MIRROR

How do your relationships mirror back to you?

254

RISK

Describe what happened to those around you
when you took a risk.

255

RISK

Describe what happened to you
when *you* took a risk.

256

COMMUNITY

Describe your ideal community. Write or draw it.

257

LOVE

Write about all the love in your life.

258

LOVE

Journal on your gratitude at knowing you are loved.

259

MIRROR

What do you want to see in the mirror?

260

MIRROR

What do you **not** want to see.

261

LINK

Describe your links in life.

262

LINK

Visit your thoughts on linking spring with re-birth.

263

LINK

Write about links offering new beginnings.

264

CONNECTION

Is there someone you need to re-connect with?

265

CONNECTION

Write about your relationships
and what links you together.

266

DISTRACTIONS

Identify distractions
and creativity zappers for you.

267

DISTRACTIONS

Spend 15 minutes today
working on removing distractions by writing.

268

OPEN

Life is also about being open to receive...
(finish this statement).

269

OPEN

What opportunities have recently opened up for you?

270

OPEN

Journal on how you can be more open with others.

271

BREATH

When I catch my breath, I will...
(finish this statement).

272

BREATHE

Breathe in creativity today and chronicle the journey.

273

LOVE

Today, love for the love of it.

274

CIRCLES

Today, draw circles around everything.

275

ABUNDANCE

What would you like more of in your life?

276

ABUNDANCE

Take a step toward creating abundance in your life.

277

SILENCE

Just for today,
eliminate all the noise and sound stimulation.

278

SILENCE

Write about the silence and how quiet it is.

279

INSPIRATION

Think of something that inspires you and draw it.

280

INSPIRATION

I am most inspired when...
(finish this statement).

281

DISTRACTIONS

I am most distracted when...
(finish this statement).

282

CONNECTION

Get out and about today,
and connect with someone new.

283

DIRT

Mud pies, sand castles or dirt forts...
which one did you create as a child?
Journal about it for 15 minutes.

284

STILLNESS

What is the meaning of stillness in your life?

285

MUSE

What inspires you to be a creative muse today?

286

JOURNAL

What good habits do you incorporate
into your daily journaling practice?

287

MEMORIES

When wearing something "Vintage,"
what memories does it invoke?

288

POSTCARD

Send a postcard today to someone
who would not expect to hear from you.

289

TRAVEL

Write about an all-expense paid trip to anywhere
and spending 6 months at that location.

290

INVISIBLE

What would you be able to see if your were invisible
that you wouldn't see if you were visible?

291

WRITE

Just for today,
write often with your non-dominant hand,
especially in your journal.

292

SHAPE

Draw a shape for today.
Use that shape throughout your day.

293

LETTER

Write a letter about a blossoming relationship
you've had in your life.
Safely keep it in your journal.

294

PAPER

Create your own special paper with color,
embellishments and designs.
Use it frequently.

295

COLOR

What's your favorite color for today?
Look for it everywhere.

296

LINK

Define a link and the links you have in your life.

297

LOVE

Put love around everything today,
and see the difference that it makes.

298

MORE

What would you like more of in your life?
Write about it today.

299

WISH

If you were granted one wish,
what would it be and why?

300

AIR

Breathe deeply today,
and enjoy the fresh air you are giving your lungs.

301

JUDGMENT

Breathe in creativity,
and exhale any judgment around your writing.

302

FAITH

I have faith and believe that...
(finish this statement).

303

POSSIBILITIES

With faith all things ... (finish this statement).

304

SHAPE

If trust was a shape, what shape would it be?

305

ORANGES

How many words can you find in just this one word?
A little hint... almost 70!

306

COSTUME

What was your favorite costume as a kid, *and* what role does that costume play in your life today?

307

FULL MOON

A full moon
offers lots of memories to muse about.
Write about a few today.

308

HAPPY

What makes you happy today?

309

HAPPINESS

Describe in detail how you make your own happiness.

310

TODAY

Write with both your dominant
and non-dominant hands - simultaneously.

311

SONG

With a song in my heart I sing my song
that I came here today to sing.

312

TRUST

Is there someone you need to trust?
Write about it.

313

TRUST

How do you trust the Greater Power to provide?

314

PATIENCE

Describe a time when your patience was tried.

315

PATIENCE

I am most patient when...
(finish this statement).

316

FAITH

If faith was a color, what color would it be today?

317

WAR

How has war affected your life...
whether world wars or your own internal war?

318

POSSIBILITIES

Dwell in all the possibilities today.

319

NOTICE

Notice 3 new things today,
that you have never noticed before.

320

PLAY

Spend a few minutes
tearing pictures from a magazine,
and collage them into your journal.

321

PLAY

Draw a shape
that keeps appearing in your life.
Color it as well.

322

JOURNAL

Journal today by writing for 20 minutes
about how journaling has changed your life.

323

WRITING

Use colored gel inks today for all your writing including your journal, to do list, even work projects.

324

QUIT

Write about a time
you quit something important.

325

RÉSUMÉ

Write about your latest accomplishment
to include on your résumé.

326

INFINITY

While writing today,
include the word "Infinity" as a theme.

327

ENCHANTMENT

Describe your definition of enchantment.

328

GRATITUDE

Each night for the next week,
write 3-5 things you are grateful for that day.

329

MUSIC

What is the song in your heart today?
Write the lyrics.

330

WHEELS

Where are the wheels of life taking you?

331

WHEEL

Draw a creativity wheel,
and list all your creative projects for the month.

332

TEARS

Describe when tears healed the hurt.

333

JOY

Define the meaning of joy in your life.

334

HONOR

What are you doing to honor your spirit today?

335

DANCE

When did you last dance?
Write about your dancing experience.

336

TRADITIONS

What family traditions have you continued
during the holidays?

337

CHILD

Watch a child's curiosity with his/her surroundings.

338

CHILD

Honor your inner child's sense of play today.

339

WALK

Notice something that you've never noticed before on your next walk.

340

TAKE A MINUTE

Take a minute and breathe - deeply.

341

LIFE

Life is what you make it.
Are you making it all that it can be?

342

AWARENESS

Journal about your awareness
of sounds you don't hear.

343

CHANGE

Consider eliminating individuals in your life
with addictive or abusive behavior.
Write about how such individuals affect your life.

344

IMAGINE

Journal on the word and all its possibilities.

345

PROCRASTINATION

What are you putting off until tomorrow?

346

CLEARING SPACE

What new things came into your life
as a result of clearing space?

347

DISTRACTIONS

How would life be different
without distractions in your life?

348

DROWNING

List 3-5 ways you can "bounce to the surface"
and eliminate that drowning feeling.

349

IMPORTANT

Remind yourself today
how important a certain someone is to you.

350

GARDEN

Visit your favorite garden and savor all the colors.

351

LAUGH

Find something that really makes you laugh with deep-in-the-belly laughter.

352

LAUGH

Today make someone else laugh.

353

MEMORIES

Make a quick sketch (or write)
about your childhood memories.

354

PASSION

If your passion was a season,
write about the season of your passion.

355

HUM

Hum your favorite song today.

356

STRETCH

Stretch your imagination today
when using your journal,
and use color or embellishments.

357

DARKNESS

Write about the darkness of the winter solstice.

358

SUNSHINE

Journal on how you make others feel when you smile.

359

SUNSHINE

Today, smile so you can be sunshine to another.

360

LIGHT

Describe the meaning of light.

361

SPARKLE

Lights, camera, action! Today is your day to sparkle!

362

TOXINS

Today, read the ingredients in all your foods.

363

TOXINS

What toxins are in your household cleaners?

364

TOXINS

What toxins do you want to eliminate?

365

PASSION

If every word has a meaning,
and every meaning has a reason,
what reason does your passion have?

ABOUT THE AUTHOR

A native of Southern New Jersey, Rosemary Augustine spent most of her adult life living in Europe, California and later, 20 years in Colorado. She returned to the Philadelphia area in 2001. However, when Rosemary relocated from Denver to the New Jersey / Pennsylvania area, something different happened besides a change of address. Rosemary embraced the culture of the northeast with a flair for creativity that opened new directions for her as an artist and author.

Rosemary spent 20 years in Corporate America and another 20 years helping people transition out of it. During her days in Corporate, she hired, managed and trained individuals. She worked for such companies as Integrated Resources, The Coach Store, Prudential Insurance and Twentieth Century-Fox Film Corporation. Beginning in 1980, she spent 10 years in the financial services industry, holding a NASD Series 7 Stock Broker's License and later worked as Director of Investor Relations for a Denver-based brokerage firm.

Rosemary continues to joke today about how she ever survived Corporate America – especially 20 years! But that all changed in 1990 when she decided it was time to become an entrepreneur and forget all the corporate craziness.

Rosemary began working as a Career Coach in 1991. She has numerous accolades awarded her as an author, coach, facilitator and speaker. Her proudest include listings in Who's Who of American Women, Who's Who in the World, and of course, being an author. Rosemary released her first book in 1995 titled *Facing Changes In Employment*, and released her second book titled *How To Live and Work Your Passion* in 2000. Through these books and her websites, she continues to inspire others to find and follow their passion.

Rosemary calls herself a Journal Aficionado - her PA License Plate reads: "Journal." She offers many creative workshops focused on art-filled play and writing taking your creative spirit to new levels. Her artistic endeavors include acrylic and watercolor painting, designing and developing hand-crafted journals as well as a daily writing practice. Rosemary helps you get focused through an age-old medium that generates ideas and opens doors never imagined – all through creativity – using art and writing as the base.

Many people feel they are not creative, and have a great fear around using paint, crayons or around journaling their thoughts. Whether working with someone changing careers or expanding an existing one, Rosemary has a unique ability to put you at ease with simple right-brain – and sometimes thought-provoking – exercises that result in pure creative expression.

Rosemary maintains an active web presence with her websites: www.RosemaryAugustine.com and www.CareerAdvice.com. She facilitates two www.MeetUp.com Groups: Journaling Circles and Self Publishing for Writers, and can also be found on Twitter at 365Days2Journal. She offers ongoing workshops and individual instruction in the areas of art, writing and publishing. Rosemary continues to provide career coaching when clients request help in their transition.

Rosemary is the owner of Blue Spruce Publishing and began her writing and consulting business in 1991. She operates her life from a 2nd story flat in Berwyn, PA along with two feisty felines named Ziggy and Zack - each an inspiration for her art and writing. She can be reached at 610.647.8863 or info@RosemaryAugustine.com.

~ ~ ~

SPECIAL THANKS

A special thanks to my friend and editor, Katherine McKay, for keeping me on the "straight and narrow" with grammar and punctuation. A special thanks to my brother, Chris, for his ongoing love, support and special humor, helping us both get through trying days. And a special thanks to all my friends and extended family, in California, Colorado, New Jersey, Pennsylvania and other parts of the USA, who love and support me unconditionally. Without all of these people, this book would not have been possible. Thank You!